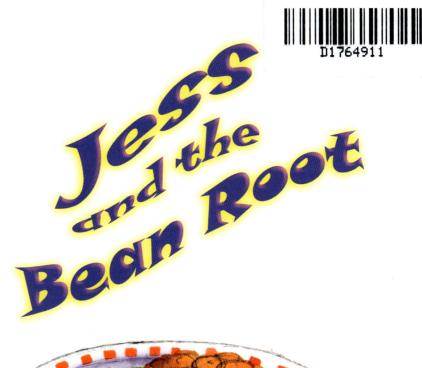

# Jess and the Bean Root

Story by Ruth Morgan
Pictures by Barbara Vagnozzi

OXFORD
UNIVERSITY PRESS

Jess lived with her mum at the top of a block of flats in a busy street. Outside, there was nowhere safe to play.

Jess spent a lot of time reading. One evening she read the story of Jack and the Beanstalk.

"Wow," thought Jess. "Jack was very lucky. Nothing like that could ever happen to me!"

At suppertime, Jess was eating
beans on toast, and thinking about
the story. Suddenly, she saw a
sparkling golden bean on her fork!
"Wow, look Mum," she said. "A
golden bean! It could be a magic
bean, like the ones in *Jack and the
Beanstalk!*"

3

Jess took the bean and ran out onto the balcony.

"Stop," said her mum. "What are you doing?"

"I'm going to plant my magic bean in the flower pot," said Jess. "It will grow into a giant beanstalk, like Jack's."

Jess dug a hole and dropped the golden bean into it, then covered it with earth.

"You silly girl," said Jess's mum. "We could have sold that bean for a lot of money! You must find it!"

Jess looked and looked for the bean, but she couldn't find it.

"I'm sorry Mum," she said.

"You can look for it again in the morning," her mum replied.

Jess went to bed, feeling very sad.

Sorry, Mum.

In the middle of the night, Jess woke up. She could hear a noise. The noise went "**Thump, Thump, Thump!**"

"My beanstalk is growing after all!" Jess thought. "I'm going to climb it, all the way up to the giant's castle." She jumped out of bed in excitement.

Thump, Thump, Thump!

Jess ran out onto the balcony
and looked up into the sky.
There was no beanstalk. Jess
was disappointed but she
could still hear the noise.
Where was it coming from?

The noise went, "Thump,
Thump, Thump". It was getting
quieter and quieter. Jess
looked down. What a
surprise she got!

There was a huge root
growing down through the floor
of the balcony. It had made a
huge hole. Now it was thumping its
way down through all the balconies of
all the flats underneath. That was the
noise that Jess had heard.

9

"I wonder where the
bean root is going?"
thought Jess. "I'd better go
down it and see."
    Jess jumped onto the bean
root and slid down,

down,

down,

going faster

and faster.

Down, down she slid until she landed, **bump**,
on the ground. The bean root didn't stop
there, it had thumped its way through the
ground, too. Jess looked at the huge hole.
    "Where's it going now?" Jess wondered. "I'd
better go down it and see."

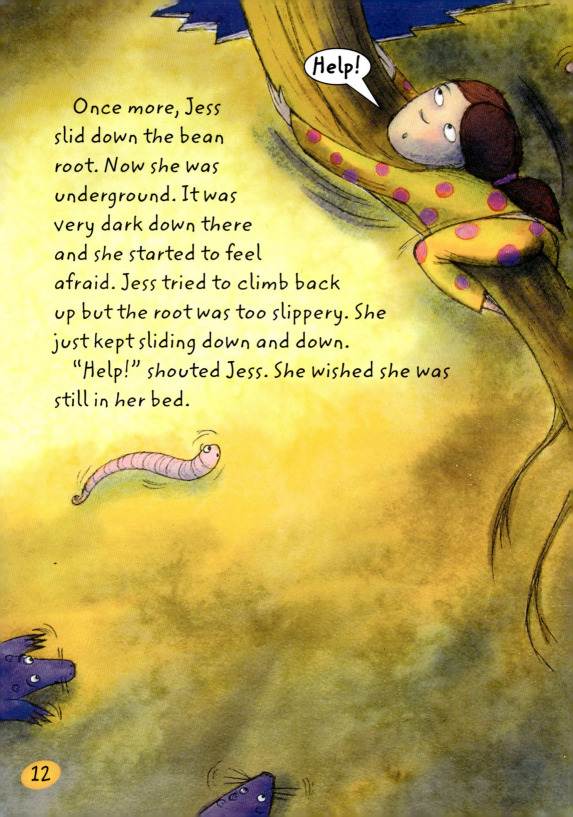

Help!

Once more, Jess slid down the bean root. Now she was underground. It was very dark down there and she started to feel afraid. Jess tried to climb back up but the root was too slippery. She just kept sliding down and down.

"Help!" shouted Jess. She wished she was still in her bed.

Suddenly Jess slid off the end of the bean root and landed on the floor with a **thump**.

She could see a little light at the end of a tunnel. Jess crept towards the flickering light, very slowly.

Jess came to a cave. In the middle of the cave there was a **huge** castle, but it looked very old and dirty.

"This must be where the giant lives," thought Jess. "I must be careful." The door of the castle was open, so Jess crept inside.

Jess came into a room that was dirty and dusty. Everything seemed to be broken. A giant was fast asleep in a chair by the fire. The giant was saying something in his sleep but Jess couldn't hear what it was. She crept a bit closer to the giant.

The giant looked very sad. He was talking to himself.

"Fee Fi Fo Fum,
I want a friend,
 Won't anyone come?"

Suddenly Jess needed to sneeze. The dust had got up her nose.

"A. A..A...Atishoo!" sneezed Jess.

The giant woke up suddenly, and fell off his broken chair.

Jess tried to run away but the giant put out a great, hairy hand to stop her.

"Please will you be my friend?" the giant asked. "I never see anyone down here. I just sleep all day because I feel so sad. My name is Hugo."

Jess didn't feel afraid now. She felt sorry for the giant.

"I'll be your friend," she said.

17

Up at the flats it was breakfast time. Everyone was surprised to see the bean root. They didn't know what it was. They looked at the holes in the balconies. Then they came down to look at the **huge** hole in the ground.

Jess's mum was very upset. She wanted to know where Jess had gone but nobody had seen her.

Suddenly, everyone heard a noise. The noise was getting louder. The ground was starting to shake.

"Get out of the way," somebody shouted. "There's something down there, under the ground!"

The ground started to crack. Everyone ran back inside.

19

A piece of the bean root burst out of the ground with Jess hanging on to it. Lots of earth flew up into the air. There was a lot of dust and everyone started sneezing.

Jess came scrambling out of the hole. Her mum was so happy to see her, she hugged and hugged her.

"Look," a man said. "There's an old castle down in that hole!"

"A giant lives there," said Jess. "Don't be afraid. His name is Hugo. He is very friendly but he is very poor. I think we should help him."

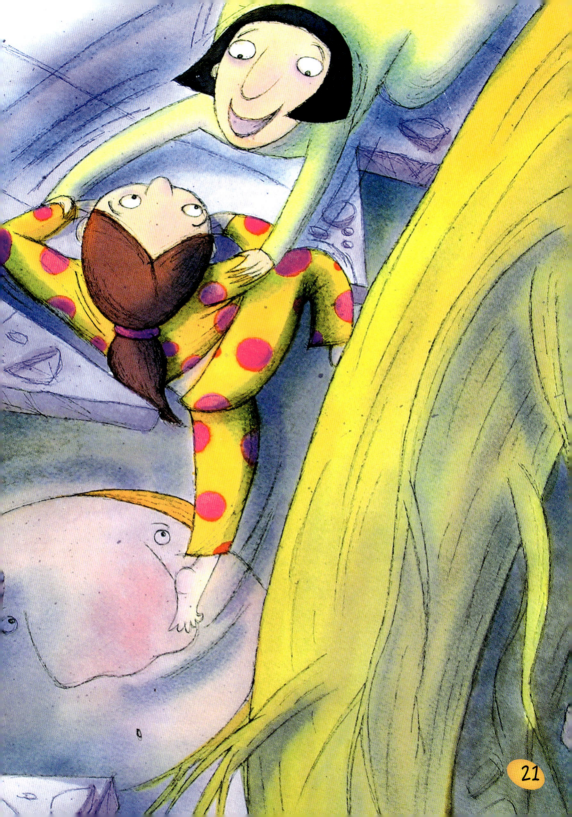

At first, the people from the flats were afraid of Hugo, but they soon got to like him. Before long, everyone was helping Hugo. They helped to paint his castle and mend his furniture. They made him new clothes and cooked him good food.

"Thank you, my friends," Hugo said.

Hugo liked the children best of all. He let them play in the castle and in his new garden.

22

23

Hugo helped the people in the flats, too. Soon, all the balconies were mended.

Hugo was very happy. He had lots of good friends but his very best friend was Jess.

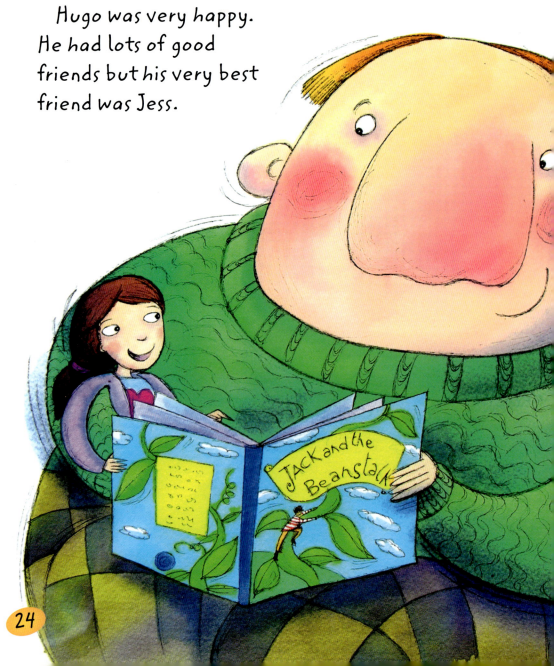

Jack and the Beanstalk